ETERNITY AWAITS:
A True Story of One Man's Journey

Jen,

I hope you find this book a blessing
and I pray God blesses you and
your family all the days of your life.

Shiloe Steinmetz

Eternity Awaits:
A True Story of One Man's Journey

Copyright © 2019 by Shiloe Steinmetz

Printed in The United States of America

Dedication

This book is dedicated to my sons Kellen and Reis, my pride and joy. Outside of Salvation in Christ, you both are my greatest joy and accomplishment in life. This book is dedicated to you as a token of my love that I may share what I have learned over the years about what God teaches us all through living out life's lessons.

Table of Contents

Preface

I decided to write this book after sitting down one evening when I had some time to think and reflect on my life. I pondered some of the major events that have taken place over the years. I have been through some major trials in my life as well as major victories; and I was reflecting on how God has been there through them all, and how he has delivered me and taught me some very valuable lessons along the way. I wanted to share some of these experiences and lessons that I have learned to show the truths of God's grace along that path.

Although everyone will have trials and tribulations throughout their entire life, I am going to share some of my experiences in my adult life, mostly as they have the greatest impact. These lessons and truths can be valuable tools for growing as a person and in faith. I will cover some major events that have had the greatest impact in my life, and brought me to where I am today. I will show how God was there the entire time, and how he has revealed his truth as he taught me in those instances.

I would like to thank my family for their love and support, and for always being there for me. My Mom, for all her help throughout the years and the unconditional love that she has shown all of us boys. My Dad, for all his hard work and the sacrifices that have allowed me some of the opportunities in life that a lot of young kids do not have. Joseph Byler, for lighting the fire under me to get this book completed. All my teachers and coaches I have had throughout the years who helped develop me and teach me all that I know today. All the Godly role models that I have had over the years who have taught me about God and his will for my life. And finally, my Heavenly father, for all the gifts in my life, including his only begotten son Jesus Christ for the salvation that he provides through his unfailing love and sacrifice on the cross.

Introduction

Everyone who has lived long enough will go through difficult times, and will soon realize that life is not easy. It is not all cupcakes and rainbows; the daily grind of life can become so cumbersome that we want to give up or go crawl under a rock and hibernate. We will go through times when we wonder if God is there; is he even listening to our prayers at all? Why would God let me go through this mess? What good could possibly ever come from the situation that I am in now? This book is for those who are struggling with some of those very questions and who may be wondering about their eternal future.

I am, for the most part, your average Joe living an average life. I have been through some very tough times, and I have also experienced some great times. I have experienced the highest of highs and the lowest of lows. Life really is like a roller coaster at times, and certainly unpredictable from day to day. It took me 47 years to write this book because that is how long it took to acquire enough life experiences to know that no matter what, no matter how many good times or bad times you have, God is there through them all. And if you pay attention and listen to that ever-small voice, you can hear God talk to you; and there is always a lesson to learn from each experience. There is a Biblical truth that can be learned from each experience because God has a purpose for everything we do, and a purpose for each of our lives. No matter how small or big you are in the scope of things, God truly does have a purpose for you and he loves you beyond your comprehension.

Until we know our true purpose in life, we will never have a lasting or meaningful joy that we were intended to have. We were made for a reason, and each of us has a destiny we were created to fulfill. We cannot know true happiness and joy until we are fulfilling that purpose in life.

I hope you enjoy this journey of one man's life experiences, and the trials and tribulations that were overcome along the way—and the victories on the other side. I hope you will see how God can teach us valuable truths from each experience we encounter in life. I also hope this book inspires you to think about your eternal future. After all, eternity awaits us all.

May God bless you.

A God wise enough to create me and the world I live in is wise enough to watch out for me.

— Philip Yancey

CHAPTER #1

When Life Runs You Over

We have all been there. We've all had times when we just feel like life is a Mack truck and just runs us over. We feel like it is impossible to get back up, and we are physically and emotionally drained. Later in the book I will show how life events can have a physical and emotional toll; but in this chapter, I want to cover something a little different.

As I had mentioned in the Introduction, I wanted to share some personal life events from my adult life that could have been life-changing or that were life-changing. But before I do that, let me share one from my youth. A long time ago, before the dinosaurs (joking, of course), I was a young boy about the age of three. From what I gathered from my parents, I tended to wander off and not listen to my parents, and do my own thing. Of course, I was too young to really remember anything, so I had to base the details on what my parents told me.

I lived in Tiffin, Ohio at the time, in a small house right in front of the Ballreich's potato-chip factory. I was very lucky to have a history with that factory because my great-grandfather Carl Ballreich and his brother Fred started the company in the very house that I was living in at the time. The factory was later built right behind the homes that were on Ohio Avenue. When Carl and Fred passed, the company was handed over to their children. One of them as was my grandmother, Phyllis Reis.

Her husband (and my grandfather), Robert Reis, worked at the plant and was a vital part of its daily operations. "Oppy", as I liked to call him, was a very special grandfather and one whom everyone loved to be around, myself especially. I would often sneak out of the house and wander back to the plant to see my Oppy without my parents' permission or knowledge. Of course, I was also too young to really grasp the idea of asking for permission.

On this rather normal morning, I had gone out of the house as usual; but did not go back to the factory. My dad was getting ready to leave for work in his Jeep, and he had just entered the truck and started it up. I had heard him start up the Jeep; so I ran toward the truck, probably to say goodbye to him. Of course, my parents both thought I was safe and sound in the house.

As I ran to the truck, I stumbled and fell behind it; and was now out of sight of my dad, who was backing out of the driveway. Before I could react, the rear tire backed over my thigh. Luckily, my mom saw me and yelled out to my father, who remembered hearing a "thud" as he backed out.

Long story short, I was taken to the hospital; and an X-ray was performed. It was confirmed that I had no broken bones and was okay. I was just a little bruised up and in pain, and it could have been much worse. I could have been killed; but by the grace of God, I was spared and here to tell this story today. This was the first time in my life when God had protected me and taught me a valuable lesson in life.

God does not give us his commandments to be some sort of dictator from above. He does not want to govern us with an iron fist, and crush us the minute we disobey one of his rules. I think sometimes, we view God in this manner and have a totally distorted view of him and who he really is. To the person who does not know the true nature of God, he may appear as a vengeful and all-powerful God who punishes those who do not obey his commands. But this could not be further from the truth.

Think about the story I just told you. Did my parents make rules and prohibit me from leaving the house without their permission to restrict me? To rule over me, just because they could? No, not at all! They did this because they love me beyond words; and wanted to protect me from the evil and dangers in the world, things that are seen and unseen, and (in this case) from trucks that are backing out that could have potentially killed me.

In the same fashion, our heavenly father gives us his commandments or rules for life not because he wants to burden us with a bunch of rules and regulations, but because he loves us and wants to protect us from all sorts of dangers. His law was given through Moses and passed down to us to protect us. His will—recorded in the scriptures by the prophets, disciples, and apostles—was given to protect us from harm. God truly wants to protect us from things seen and unseen; has wisdom beyond comprehension; and knows exactly what we need and exactly what could harm us mentally, physically, and spiritually.

When we do not listen to God and disobey his commands, we are not only sinning against him, but we are hurting ourselves as well. I look back at every instance in my life where I disobeyed God and his will for me, and I found that I only ended up hurting myself down the road. Now that I have the luxury of hindsight, I wish I obeyed then. One scripture that really stands out and that bears so much truth is Galatians 6:7-8 (NIV): *"Do not be deceived: God cannot be mocked. A man reaps what he sows. Whoever sows to pleasure their flesh, from the flesh will reap destruction; whoever sows to please the Spirit, from the Spirit will reap eternal life."*

3

Think about that for a minute. What God is really saying is if you do bad things, you can expect bad things to result from your actions. Likewise, if you do good things, then you can expect good things to eventually come your way. Who really wants bad things to happen to them? No one, but that is exactly what we are setting ourselves up for when we sin against God. It is kind of like setting yourself up for "self-destruct" mode.

Let me give you an example so you can see how the sowing-and-reaping concept may work in the real world. Let's say you are married and are out with your friends one night and have had way too much to drink. Someone of the opposite sex starts flirting with you and you think there is no harm in it, so you willingly flirt back. Next thing you know, you're leaving with that person and end up in a situation that you never intended. Later, your spouse finds out or you come clean; and suddenly you find yourself headed to divorce court. Worse yet, if you have children, they are affected by your sin. In the following years, you experience loneliness, financial trouble, separation from your kids, and all the other painful things that come with divorce.

Here's another example. We live a very unhealthy lifestyle. We abuse our body by drinking too much, smoking several packs of cigarettes a day, and eating very poorly; and we are severely overweight. Because these are all things God deters us from doing and are not in his will for us, we again sow of the flesh and will eventually reap its consequences. We may end up with heart problems from our poor eating habits, lung cancer from all the smoking, or alcoholism years down the road.

Reflecting on these two examples, I want to remind you that God can turn things around and make good of what we have done, and will always forgive a true repentant heart. But this does not mean he will always take away the consequences of what we have done.

In summary, it is always in our best interest to listen to God and obey his word to avoid troubles that we cannot see. His "rules" and commandments are for our protection, so take advantage of this protection that God offers from his infinite wisdom and word.

The safest place in all the world is in the will of God, and the safest protection in all the world is the name of God.

— Warren Wiersbe

> As soon as you willfully allow a dialogue with temptation to begin, the soul is robbed of peace, just as consent to impurity destroys grace.
>
> Josemaría Escrivá

CHAPTER #2

Don't Rob Yourself!

Reminder: Let nothing steal your joy. Let nothing kill your peace.[1]

We have all had those times in our life when we wish we could turn back the hands of time and change things from our past. How nice would it be if we could make changes to our past from the knowledge we have now? After all, they always say hindsight is 20/20; if we knew what we know now, life would be much different. There may be things we have done in our past that we are ashamed of, or decisions we made that currently affect us negatively. And of course, the consequences from those past events can linger many years into the future.

We learn from and grow through some of the mistakes we have made. For example, when we were young and touched a hot stove, we immediately knew we would never do that again because of the pain and burn that it gave us. We recovered and learned from that past mistake, and have been much more careful around a hot stove going forward.

But other mistakes are so severe, some never recover from them, or are able to carry on a normal life afterward. Some mistakes are not so forgiving—like the guy who goes drinking with his buddies one night and has one too many, then attempts to drive home.

---

1 "Let Nothing Steal Your Joy". LiveLifeHappy.com, https://livelifehappy.com/life-quotes/let-nothing-steal-joy/.

On his way home from the bar, it's raining and it's hard to see anything outside. Unfortunately, he accidentally hits a pedestrian walking on the road and kills him. Then the police arrive and discover he was drinking. Next thing he knows, he is charged with vehicular homicide. A trial ensues, and he finds himself in prison.

That is one decision that will cost him much more than he ever imagined; and I am sure that if he could change his past, he would. Let's face it, we all have things we would go back in time for and change if we could. I know I have a few, for sure.

I would like to share one of those times with you, and what I learned from it.

I was about fifteen years old; and of course, I thought I was invincible. One thing I was really into at that time was rock music, and especially loved to listen to '80s metal hair bands. I had a pretty good collection, but always wanted to add to it.

For some reason, on this regrettable day, I was with a friend who had shoplifted in the past. We were in the record store at the mall. He was much more experienced in the "five-finger discount" arena, and had convinced me to try it. I figured no one was looking, it would save me money, and I could get more tapes. I reasoned myself into doing it, and thought I would never get caught.

I then picked up a tape and stuck it down my pants when I thought no one was looking. To my surprise and bad luck, there just happened to be an off-duty police officer in the store that day. Next thing I knew, I had a hand on my shoulder and was being walked back to a small office where management apprehended thieves. After a phone call, a police officer was there and taking me away in the back of his car to the downtown police station. Once there, I had to make the dreaded call to my parents to come pick me up.

I was ashamed and mad at myself at the same time for doing something I knew was wrong, and now I would have to live up to the consequences. I ended up having to go to court and stand in front of the judge, give an account of my actions, and face the sentence that was due. Luckily, in this case, the judge was very merciful. I left with 50 hours of community service, as well as a very bruised ego.

The irony of the whole thing was that the cassette tape I stole was by a band named Stryper. If anyone remembers that band from the '80s, they were a self-proclaimed Christian metal band. How sad of a story is that? Stealing a Christian band's cassette tape... kind of contradictory, don't you think? I did learn some very valuable life lessons from the whole thing, and discovered that it is never worth the pain you must go through. Doing what you know is wrong only steals joy and peace from you in the end. In my case, it was not me stealing from the music store; it was my actions stealing much more from me.

God gave us a list of commandments that we know now are there to really protect us. The 8th commandment, "Thou shall not steal", is to protect us from a variety of consequences that come with that sin. We not only hurt ourselves when we steal; we also hurt others. God, in his infinite wisdom, loves all creation and gave this commandment to protect us emotionally, physically, and spiritually. Because God is omniscient, he sees and knows all things. We never really "get away" with anything in the end.

Just like I thought I would get away with shoplifting, I found out the hard way that wasn't the case. As we soon will find out, we never get away with sin because God does sees all, and we will have to give an account someday of all we have done. Facing the judge on that day without the grace and work of Jesus Christ will be a terrifying experience.

You may think you may get away with sin because no one will ever know; that is a lie that Satan wants you to believe. So, when temptation comes to do something we know is wrong, or if we reason that there's nothing wrong with doing a little thing if it doesn't hurt anyone, we must think about what we are doing, what consequences it could have, and if God would approve of it. All of these are things to think about when we are tempted to sin and think we will get away with it.

As we have seen now, there are instances in life where when our actions or attitudes rob us of peace and joy, like stealing. There are also other things we do or things we hold on to that rob us of peace and joy. Bitterness and unforgiveness are things many of us hold on to, and they also rob us of many good things in our lives.

I want to share a story that comes from my family history where this was the case. The family was damaged when bitterness and unforgiveness showed its ugly face. My great-grandfather Carl and his brother Fred started a potato-chip factory in Tiffin, Ohio in 1920, and it blossomed over time into a thriving business. If you have never tried Ballreich's potato chips, you should try them; they are the best chips around. I am a little biased, of course. But honestly, they are truly unique.

As time passed, Carl and Fred had children and eventually passed the business on to them. Then as they aged, the business was naturally transitioned to their children. As more time passed, the business would be transitioned again. But this time, it wasn't as easy as it was then. To make a long story short, some of the siblings thought a very unfair deal had resulted. This led to bitterness and anger between my grandmother and her two brothers, who were also Carl's children. Sadly, my grandmother and her brothers did not talk for over twenty years, and it wasn't until one of her brothers was in his last days that he finally made peace with my grandmother. For all those years, they held resentment and robbed themselves of the joy of family that could have been in the twenty years prior.

Far too often, we let hurt feelings turn into unforgiveness. This divides friendships and families. The Bible has a lot to say about forgiveness, and it is a major theme. God forgave us when we sinned against him and turned away from him; so likewise, he commands us to do the same: *"Be kind and compassionate to one another, forgiving each other, just as in Christ God forgave you."* (Ephesians 4:32 NIV) Without forgiveness, we hold on to emotions that only hurt us in the end and rob us of true happiness.

But you may ask, "How can I forgive someone who has mistreated me repeatedly and for years, and how often should I forgive them? That is a great question because it is very difficult to forgive someone who has repeatedly done you wrong. The answer is found in Matthew 18:21-22 (NIV): *"Lord, how many times shall I forgive my brother or sister who sins against me? Up to seven times?" Jesus answered, 'I tell you, not seven times, but seventy-seven times.'"*

So you see, Jesus tells us we must forgive each other; and goes a step further and tells us we must do it repeatedly if we must. God always sets the example before he gives such a command. Think about it for a moment. If we sinned against God and he then forgives us, what would happen if we sinned against him again (we all do) and he didn't forgive us a second or third time? We would all end up in hell, eternally separated from God, because we blew it. God forgives us time and time again, over and over, and expects us to do the same to others. God, in his infinite wisdom, knows that unforgiveness does more harm to the one who withholds forgiveness than the one who is unforgiven. It is like a cancer that will eat you from the inside out if not dealt with. It leads to bitterness, which eventually leads to regret.

How many people can you think of who were on their death beds and wished they forgave someone they didn't? Often, they wished they could have back a relationship they let be destroyed by bitterness and unforgiveness. They lived their lives holding on to something that only imprisoned them.

> *To forgive is to set a prisoner free and discover that*
> *the prisoner was you.*
>
> — *Lewis B. Smedes*

Don't live your life with regrets; and don't hold on to bitterness from not forgiving someone while you still can go take the first step and make peace and forgive, or ask for forgiveness. You will feel better in the end, and know you did everything you could to make amends. You should do everything in your power to make that first step. If the person you forgive or ask forgiveness from turns away from your offer, it now falls on them. Romans 12:18 (ESV) says, *"If possible, so far as it depends on you, live peaceably with all."* From this verse, we see that it depends on us to take that step, and do everything in our power to make peace. Don't rob yourself of peace and joy by harboring bitterness and unforgiveness. Most importantly, do not do anything that you know will rob you of the joy that God wants for us all.

CHAPTER #3

Burned Out

The greatest legacy one can pass on to one's children and grandchildren is not money or other material things accumulated in one's life, but rather a legacy of character and faith.

— *Billy Graham*

Okay, so we have all heard of the term "burned out" before, and many of us have been there. Life can be very demanding and can put a lot of pressure on us. The daily grind of work, school, kids, home maintenance, bills, you name it… All these things take their toll on us, and can cause burnout. We always need to find that right balance in life so we don't reach that dreaded state. That is a whole different topic I could write about for days, but I would like to share a slightly different story with you of a time in my life when I was literally burned out.

It was right after Christmas in 1998, and my wife and I were spending the night relaxing and enjoying a movie at home. Life was pretty good: I was young and had a very nice house, and filled it with a lot of nice furniture and things I had acquired over a short period of time. I was proud of myself for being so young and accumulating a lot of material things. After all, many people in my same age group were still working on independence and living at home with their parents.

Anyway, as we sat there watching a movie with a nice fire going in the fireplace, things soon took a drastic change for the worse. At first, we heard a very peculiar noise that sounded like someone was taking a metal sheet and shaking it violently. It was a very unique sound, so that was what first drew our attention. Then a small dark circle appeared just above the mantle on the fireplace, and it started to grow bigger and bigger. Then the light bulb went off in my head, and I knew right away what was happening.

In a panic, I thought that if I could get to the fire inside the wall before it spread and put it out, I could control the damage. I dashed over to the wall and looked for something to punch it with to get to the fire inside. I could not find anything, so I clenched my fist and punched. My fist easily went through the wall; and as soon as it did, I knew I made a huge mistake. I just gave the fire the air it needed to fuel its destructive power. A ball of flames flew out toward me, and I realized it was already too late.

At that point, it was now a mad dash to call the fire department and try to get the most valuable things out of our home. The first thing we did after making that call was get our two Doberman Pinschers, Roxie and Ozzie, out of the house and take them over to the neighbors. Next, we grabbed photo albums and irreplaceable items, and threw them onto the front yard. In the process, when I was outside, I noticed that the fire on the roof had rapidly swept across the ventilation and to the other side. We were making back-and-forth trips as rapidly as we could as the smoke became intense.

Although it seemed like an eternity, the fire department arrived only a few moments later. They started watering down the neighbors' houses before engulfing ours in gallons and gallons of water. Once the flames were under control, they methodically started knocking holes into all the walls to find any remnants of smoldering flames. The house was totaled, as well as everything left inside it.

In all the excitement, I had not realized how much smoke I had inhaled. I soon found myself being brought by ambulance to the nearby hospital, where I received oxygen and a thorough evaluation. Most of everything that I had accumulated up to that point was now in ruins, but I was thankful that everyone was safe and no lives were lost that day. We spent the next nine months living in an apartment, and had the pleasure (sarcasm) of dealing with the insurance company in trying to replace everything that was lost.

Looking back now at what happened, I can say it was a good learning experience; and realized that God had some valuable lessons from the incident.

First, God is always in control; and can take any bad situation and turn it into good. But in all of it, we were alive and thankful that we were not asleep during the fire, and nothing was lost except material things that could be replaced. The main thing I learned from the fire is that we should not place so much value on material things because they can be taken from us at any time. We should be thankful for the things we do have, and trust that God will always provide for us even when we can't see how. If we rely solely on our abilities and what we can save up, we are setting ourselves up for major disappointment and failure because life can change in the blink of an eye, and all your material things can be destroyed. Everything you have worked so hard for can be taken away in a matter of minutes. You could win the Mega Millions lottery one day and be diagnosed with terminal cancer the next day.

I have been on both sides of the coin in my life when it comes to having "stuff". In college, I lived in an older house that had burned down and was rebuilt, and still had that smoky smell. I was with four other guys and ate ramen noodles and macaroni and cheese for meals, and didn't have much money at all. Then I went to the other extreme of living in a 12,000-square-foot home that had 10 bathrooms and a full 2,000-square-foot gym in the basement, and had no debt at all.

That's going from one extreme to the other; so I can say with experience that it is not things, house size, money, or what you have that makes you happy. I was happier somewhere in the middle; but when I had what seemed like everything, I was not happy at all. We fall into that trap of trying to pursue bigger things and have more money in search of happiness. In the end, it is only a carrot on a stick. It leads to despair and takes you down a rabbit hole of endless pursuits. Real and lasting happiness only comes when you do what you were created to do, and that is to worship your creator. Whether you are rich or poor, you will always find joy and peace because your true wealth is stored up in heaven through faith.

God tells us to trust in him and place our valuables where they cannot be taken from us. Matthew 6:19-21 (NIV) reads:

Do not store up for yourselves treasures on earth, where moths and vermin destroy, and where thieves break in and steal. But store up for yourselves treasures in heaven, where moths and vermin do not destroy, and where thieves do not break in and steal. For where your treasure is, there your heart will be also.

This is a reminder from God that we should place our real treasure (our salvation and relationship with him) in the only place that is truly secure eternally. We should trust him and follow him with our whole heart. Another good reminder is found in Mark 8:36 (KJV) when Jesus tells us, *"For what shall it profit a man, if he shall gain the whole world, and lose his own soul?"*

We need to always keep our focus and seek things that really matter. After all, when we die, it does not matter how much money and things we have, how famous we are, or what we accomplished. We die and return to dust, and are certainly not taking anything with us that we have accumulated here on earth. The only thing that matters is if we know Jesus and trust in him for our salvation. It is all meaningless unless we have a personal and trusting relationship with our God.

I encourage you to start thinking about what you are really investing in, and putting your faith and trust in. Is it Jesus; or is it money, wealth, and things that are here today and gone tomorrow?

CHAPTER #4

A Brush with Death on the Iron Pony

Death is not the end, it is simply walking out of the physical form and into the spirit realm, which is our true home. It's going back home.

— Stephen Christopher

Many of us have probably heard stories from people who have had near-death experiences. The stories range from seeing a white light at the end of a tunnel to seeing themselves as they float up or hover over their own bodies. The phrase I hear quite often is, "I saw my life flash before my eyes." Most people who have never had a near-death experience may think those who have are crazy, but I can tell you for certain that most are indeed not. Well, I unfortunately had a near-death experience myself; but fortunately, I am alive today to tell you about it.

It was early spring in 2001, and I had just gotten my motorcycle out after a long winter. At this point in my life, I usually didn't care what the weather was like as I rode all the time. I was also going through a difficult time, and was not in the best state of mind on this day. I had received some very bad news a few weeks before, and was trying to deal with the aftermath.

I figured I'd go for a ride to clear my head. I would often take a ride to just relax and feel the wind go through my hair (yes, I had hair back then). This was my time to just think and reflect as I spun down the open highway. I was in a hurry that day, so I only had jeans and a t-shirt on; and of course, like many riders, no helmet.

I lived in the country at the time, and there was a road that was about 10 miles long, going from my house to the west side of Columbus. I started down the road, thinking about some of the issues that I was facing in life at that moment when I came up to a series of curves on the road. I knew this road very well because I drove it every day to and from work.

I was going maybe 60 MPH. As I approached the curve, I noticed a car that had stopped at the intersection, where the first bend in the road was. The car had a stop sign and I did not, so I assumed the car clearly saw me. As I approached, he started to pull out. Then he must have seen me at the last minute and stopped. It was just enough to startle me and take my full attention off the curves, and on to the car sitting there.

I shifted my focus back to the road in front of me, but it was too late. The curve had come faster than expected; and I was now in the gravel on the side of the road, trying to make the turn. My front tire started to rapidly sway back and forth. I tried to hold it steady, but soon found the front end of the bike going down. I knew I was now going down with it.

They say there are two types of bikers: those who have gone down, and those who eventually will. If you're a biker or have ridden for a long time, you know this is kind of a true statement. I guess this was my time to make that statement hold up.

As I went down, the bike started to tumble forward and threw me into the air. When the bike flipped over itself, I was probably going at a speed of 50-55 MPH. I braced for impact, and I clearly remember seeing a million events in my mind's eye. What seemed like an eternity were just split seconds, but I distinctly remember seeing events in my life flash through my mind. I could see myself as a young child playing baseball, then playing football in high school, then graduating from pharmacy school, and then working as a pharmacist. Finally, the last thing I recall seeing before hitting the ground was people standing in front of my casket at my funeral.

BAM! I hit the pavement at about 50 MPH, and rolled and rolled just past a telephone pole and stopped about 25 yards in a farmer's field. I remember thinking, "I am alive! Thank you, Jesus!"

The adrenaline was in full effect, and I felt nothing as I stood up. Two different cars had stopped, and the drivers rushed over to where I was standing. I remember one asking, "Are you okay?" I nodded back, then I was asked, "Do you want me to call for an ambulance?"

At this point, I looked down and started to scan my body. I remember seeing shredded pants and blood. I looked at my torn shirt that was now covered in blood as well. Then, like a bolt of lightning hitting me, the adrenaline wore off and the pain crept in as I fell to the ground.

I lay there over the next few minutes, waiting for the squad to arrive. When they did, they cautiously prepped me to lock my cervical spine in place, strapped me to the board, and lifted me into the back of the ambulance. The ride seemed like an eternity as I remember we hit every bump along the way, sending jolts of pain through my entire body. At the hospital, they did scans and X-rays and many other tests. After it all, by God's grace, I had no broken bones, no internal bleeding, and no head trauma. I only had severe road rash and a separated shoulder. I ended up having two surgeries years down the road to fix some of the damage; but on that night, I went home alive.

Lying in bed that night at home, I kept wondering how I made it. How did I not hit my head even once on the ground while going at that speed? How did I miss that telephone pole and not be split in half? How did I not have internal damage or broken bones? How am I alive? The answer to all these questions is: by God's grace. I knew I had unfinished work to do, and he still has a purpose for my life. I cannot say for certain, and maybe I was overanalyzing things after it all. But it was almost as if someone was protecting me, and someone held my head up the entire time so I did not hit it on the ground. God had to have been protecting me during that crash; there is no other explanation.

Think about your own life for a moment, and about a time when something bad like that had happened to you. Was God was working behind the scenes, even when you were not aware of it? He is always there protecting us from danger, whether you realize it or not. When parents and family pray for your health and safety, these are the times God is answering those prayers; and we are not even aware of it. Because of this experience in my life, I have learned that God is always there and always watching over us. We are his children; and like any great parent, he is continually watching over and protecting his children.

I know beyond a doubt that God answers prayers and protects those we pray for. Because I know this, I pray over my sons almost daily, asking God for his divine intercession and protection over them. When they fall asleep, I lay hands on them and pray, asking for their protection and safety. I know that God answers those prayers, and either watches over them himself or has his angels available to give them divine protection.

My son Kellen has a milder case of cerebral palsy, and has a difficult time with balance and coordination. I have seen him fall many times over the years, and miss objects that could have really hurt him. Is this coincidence, or is this again God answering those prayers and protecting his falls?

Again, this goes back to a previous point I made in an earlier chapter. You never know what tomorrow holds. You are never promised tomorrow, so invest in the things that are eternal. You can plan, you can build, and you can acquire things in life; but life can also change forever in a split second. How many of us have had friends or people we know who are here today and gone tomorrow?

Some great reminders from God that we should be thankful for each day and not boast about the future can be found in his word. Proverbs 27:1 (NIV) says, *"Do not boast about tomorrow, for you do not know what a day may bring."* Jesus also gives us a great parable in Luke 12:16-21 (NKJV) when he said:

"The ground of a certain rich man yielded plentifully. And he thought within himself, saying, 'What shall I do, since I have no room to store my crops?' So he said, 'I will do this: I will pull down my barns

and build greater, and there I will store all my crops and my goods. And I will say to my soul, "Soul, you have many goods laid up for many years; take your ease; eat, drink, and be merry." But God said to him, 'Fool! This night your soul will be required of you; then whose will those things be which you have provided?' "So is he who lays up treasure for himself, and is not rich toward God."

You can see that it does not matter how rich you are or how many things you acquire if you are not rich toward God and focus on what really matters. Never forget that what really matters is your relationship with him. God gives us plenty of reminders throughout the Bible to not focus so much on earthly things and worry about the senseless things we worry about; he is in control, and wants you to trust in him.

Most of us spend so much time trying to plan and worry about the future that we lose sight of today and the joys that God has put right in front of us. We strive to secure our own futures, and sometimes lose sight of God altogether in the process. I am not saying to forgo planning and saving for the future at all. Rather, do not let it consume you and forget to trust God for the things we need daily because he will provide for us. Don't let your heart be set on things we can accumulate, such as earthly treasures. God reminds us to store up heavenly treasure in Matthew 6:19-21 as we already learned in Chapter 3.

Take some time to reflect on these questions now: Where are you storing your treasures? Who or what are your putting your trust in? Do you have faith that God will protect and provide for you, or are you trusting in yourself and what you can do to secure your future? Your eternity by faith is already secured and, when put into perspective, should naturally bring a sense of peace and comfort. Remember that we are not promised tomorrow; life can change in the blink of an eye, so start laying up treasure and riches where they cannot be taken from you, and remember that God is always there looking over you and protecting you, even when you are not aware of it.

Back in the saddle again 12 years after accident

Reis and Kellen in front of Route 30 Harley Davidson in Upper Sandusky, Ohio. They are a big part of the Route 30 Harley Davidson Family.

Comebacks don't seem likely when your back is up against the wall and your hope is depleted. But if you will stay the course, you will discover God's power to reverse the irreversible in your life.

— *Tony Evans*

CHAPTER #5

Don't Call It a Comeback

Not all the things that have happened to me in the past that taught me valuable life lessons are bad things. In fact, there have been some awesome things that I have experienced that have also shaped who I am today. One of those things is bodybuilding!

As I reflect on the things I have achieved in the sport, I am amazed at what God has afforded me to accomplish in a relatively short period of time: two Mr. Ohio titles, two World Championships appearances, professional status in three separate drug-free organizations, two Universe Heavyweight National Titles, and over 70 contests competed in with over 40 Overall titles. I have done more than most could ever dream of in the sport. I was sponsored by a major supplement company, and appeared in magazines. I will stop there, but you get the idea: I have been blessed.

I want to share a little bit about my bodybuilding career and how I got started, and some practical life truths that I have learned along the way. I was always into exercising and keeping myself in shape, even at an early age. I remember that at my parents' house, we had a universal gym machine in our garage; and I would go out there and work out and fantasize about becoming my childhood hero, Arnold Schwarzenegger, someday. Even in college, when I could not get to the gym due to school's tedious demand and workload, I would do push-ups in my room just so I was doing something physically active for the day. But my bodybuilding journey began back in 1995, when I graduated from pharmacy School and could finally afford the nutrition and supplements I needed to grow.

I started training at World Gym in Columbus, Ohio. Anyone who is familiar with the sport knows that Columbus is a hub for physique competition. Many of the great competitive athletes in the sport of bodybuilding and fitness are from or train in Columbus. Arnold himself hosts the Arnold Classic and Fitness Expo there every year. It is the largest event of its kind in the world, and people from all over the world flock there each year for this momentous event. Because of this fact, I probably got an extra boost when starting out in the fitness arena. I really began to get into it, and had a great training partner at the time—we worked together at Merck-Medco, and he also was a pharmacist.

The manager of World Gym at the time was a great guy by the name of Mike Roberts, and he convinced me to try doing a bodybuilding show. He said to me, "Shiloe, you have great genetics and a God-given build. You should compete in a bodybuilding show." I had no idea what I was doing. But, to make a long story short, I decided to give it a go.

Soon after that, I, Mike, and another guy named Chris all went to Northern Kentucky to compete in our very first show in 1997. I was scared, but glad I did it; and will never forget seeing the guy who won the Overall title that night. I remember thinking to myself, *That guy is amazing. Wouldn't it be amazing to win an Overall title someday?* I never thought at the time that was possible for me (funny how God works; just a few years later, I was that guy), but I was hooked from that night on. I did three more contests that very same year, but did not compete again until 1999; and did only one contest then due to the demands of life. I was also adjusting to a new life after the house fire of 1998.

I eventually got the bug again and wanted to compete. I was about to start the long prep process when I received some bad news, and was delayed again. Then the fateful motorcycle accident in 2001 happened, and I thought it essentially ended my bodybuilding career. Due to recovery, surgeries, and rehab, bodybuilding was now a distant fantasy.

Time went on. I knew God had placed in me the desire to step on stage again, so I decided to make a comeback. After setting up a small gym in my basement, I started to train again. I was embarrassed to go to a real gym because I had lost so much muscle, and was weak from starting all over.

It was now 2003, and I was again fueled with passion and wanted to make a mark. The stage was set for a comeback. That year, I competed in over 21 shows all over the country, doing contests back to back, sometimes for 4 weeks in a row at a time. That was and still is unheard of. I was in several natural bodybuilding shows; and at one contest, I took second, and thought I should have won the show.

It is now standard to ask the judges for feedback, so I decided to do that and see what I could do to hit that top spot. I remember asking the head judge for feedback, and what I could do to improve. I will never forget his response: "Nothing. If you're truly natural, go professional." I thought about that for a while, and decided that was exactly what I wanted to do.

Can you start to see a common thread here yet? If not, I will just tell you plainly. The common theme is someone planting a seed, and that seed taking off and growing into something bigger. The same is true when we share the Gospel of Jesus: you never know how it is going to be received, or how it will change someone's life. Our job is just to plant the seed and let God cultivate it. It is amazing how someone would seemingly just reject your message one day, and you'll see this person later down the road and find out that the seed you planted had sprouted. Sometimes, you see a whole different person.

Now back to my bodybuilding journey. I took that seed the gym manager Mike planted to begin my journey in bodybuilding, and then the seed that the head judge planted to go out and work toward a pro card in natural bodybuilding.

A few weeks later, I entered a "pro qualifier" and won my pro card that same night. I then entered a few professional shows, and even won my very first professional show: the NGA Pro Olympus in Buffalo, New York. The following year, I did 15 contests and ventured into the non-drug-tested shows as a natural athlete, and even beat the guys who were using all sorts of performance-enhancing drugs. That was the same year I won the Overall title in the contest I was telling you about earlier when I first started out. I was now rolling high in my bodybuilding career, and winning all over the country. I won the Mr. Ohio title in 2008, as well as class wins in National-level shows. My comeback was not only complete, but I was a dominant force in the bodybuilding arena.

Then in 2011, my twin sons were born prematurely. That's when bodybuilding came to a screeching halt. Once again, the demands of life and my situation forced me to retire and leave bodybuilding pretty much all together. Unfortunately, a divorce followed a few short years later; and rebuilding my life again was the main concern, along with being a single dad and all the responsibilities and demands that came along with that.

After five long years, I still had the desire to compete. So I decided in 2016 to convert my small garage into a gym and start training again.

I was toying around with the idea of stepping on stage again after my long hiatus from the sport. The timing was finally right, and I decided to make a second comeback.

I began the prep process. After 10 weeks, the time had once again come to step on stage. I had no idea how my body would respond, or what I would look like after taking so much time off. I was a little anxious, even though I had done it dozens of times before. This was a warm-up contest in Indiana for my target contest, the Mr. Ohio contest in Columbus, to be held two weeks later. At the end of the night, I was victorious and won the Overall title. To make things sweeter, my sons were in attendance and saw their dad compete for the first time ever.

I was thrilled, but the pressure soon began as the Mr. Ohio contest loomed. The pressure was higher than ever because I was expected to be at the top, like I had been in the past. And as a former Mr. Ohio, people were probably expecting nothing less than a repeat.

I was now much older than when I won the title before; and at 44, I was just hoping to still be competitive. My family and sons were in attendance, and I wanted them to be proud. The field of athletes was very tough, but I had won the heavyweight class.

Then came the Overall comparisons. It was going to be close, and I knew it. The comparisons were judged, and the pose-down was over. Now we were lined up, just waiting for the judges' decision. I was more nervous than ever as I waited to hear the decision.

The MC received the card, and began the announcement: "Our Overall Champion and 2016 Mr. Ohio goes to... Number 54, Shiloe Steinmetz." I was overwhelmed as I knew what I had overcome to win that title again at 44, and thankful for God's grace in allowing me to overcome adversity to achieve the highest honor in the state yet again. My sons came up on stage with me for pictures, and I gave each one the trophies I had won. That was the greatest highlight of the night for me.

Why did I tell you this story? Because I believe that anyone can accomplish anything they put their mind to, and God instills in each one of us the ability to overcome adversity. We are all champions inside; we just need to believe that, and work hard to bring that champion to the surface. Call what I did a comeback or whatever you want, but I know now that it was never a comeback at all. I always had that champion inside, and God had allowed me to yet again to display what he already gave me.

Similarly, God gives us the ability to resist temptation and overcome the persecution of our faith because he is always with us. If we have the Holy Spirit living inside us, we know that we can do and accomplish all things and overcome obstacles in the world because he has also overcome the world. I am not saying that this means we can do all carnal and earthly things, but we can overcome temptation and resist the devil by the power of the one who lives inside us.

1 John 4:4 (ESV) says: *"Little Children, you are from God and have overcome them, for he who is in you is greater than he who is in the world."* Another reminder of this same concept is found in Philippians 4:13 (NKJV): *"I can do all things through Christ who strengthens me."* We can do much more and accomplish more than we think if we trust, rely on, and pray to the one who created us. If you're ever down and out, or don't think you can go on any longer in your dire situation, just remind yourself of the fact that you are never alone in your journey. God is always with you and for you; just pray and have faith, and wait and see what he will do in your life.

Like I mentioned in the beginning of this chapter, your words of encouragement can plant seeds that will grow in others. Make sure you plant seeds of hope, grace, and love that inspire and promote; and not seeds that tear down and bring despair and self-doubt. Negative words will produce negative results, but positive words bring positive results and strengthen faith. Just like Mike propelled me to compete and the rest is history, you can encourage someone else to greater things.

Most importantly, when we plant seeds, we should be planting the seeds of faith in he who provides salvation. We should tell others the good news of Jesus Christ, who has made the way for us to have eternal life. You never know who will be affected or when the seed you planted will grow in that person; it is just our job to tell the good news and plant the seed. Jesus gave us what we now know as the great commission:

Therefore go and make disciples of all nations, baptizing them in the name of the Father and of the Son and of the Holy Spirit, and teaching them to obey everything I have commanded you. And surely I am with you always, to the very end of the age. (Matthew 28:19-20 NIV)

This chapter was primarily about my "comeback" in the sport of bodybuilding and how I got started, and how some small encouraging words turned into something greater. As I pointed out, we can also give encouraging words to others when we share the Gospel of Jesus Christ and his message, and how his words can dramatically change someone's life. Sometimes, we all need a "comeback" in life because we all fall and struggle; we all can feel like we have fallen away in faith and are so far from God, we can never turn back. The truth is we are never very far from God. No matter what you have done in life or how bad a situation is, you can turn back to God at any time, under and circumstance, and from any sin.

Jesus attested to this truth by telling us the story of the Prodigal Son. This story, also known as the Parable of the Lost Son, follows immediately after the parables of the Lost Sheep and the Lost Coin. With these three parables, Jesus demonstrated what it means to be lost, how heaven celebrates with joy when the lost are found, and how the loving Father longs to save people.

The story of the Prodigal Son starts with a man who has two sons. The younger son asks his father for his portion of his inheritance now. Once he gets the money, he heads off to a distant land and begins to blow his fortune on wild and reckless living. He then runs out of money, and a famine hits the country. He then finds a job feeding pigs, and becomes so desperate that he considers eating the food that is for the pigs. The son eventually remembers his father, and how good he had it back home. He becomes humble, and decides to return to his father and ask for forgiveness. Little did he know that his father had been waiting for him to come home the whole time he was gone. When he returns home, his father receives him with open arms of compassion. Immediately, the father turns to his servants and asks them to prepare an enormous feast in celebration of his son's return. (Luke 15:11-32)

As you can see, Jesus is telling us of the love of the father; and how he longs for us to come back to him and seek his gracious forgiveness. So no matter what you have done or how long you have been away from God, he is always waiting for you to come back to him, and will receive you with open arms and forgiveness. He will never force you to return to him, but instead he will patiently wait for however long it takes for you to make your comeback.

Comeback of 2016 and 2nd Mr. Ohio Title

Yes, you see, there's no such thing as coincidence. There are no accidents in life. Everything that happens is the result of a calculated move that leads us to where we are.

— *J.M. Darhower*

CHAPTER #6

Coincidence or Not?

The next two stories I would like to share with you deal with trusting God and what his word says. We all have varying levels of faith, and we either believe or do not believe what the Bible says. God has revealed himself to us through his word or the Bible. He accomplished revealing himself through different people throughout history, such as the prophets, apostles, and disciples.

In a world of relativity, is there any absolute truth? That is a question to ponder for a moment. How often do we hear today that what is true for you may not be true for me, and you have your views and I have mine? That seems like a noble statement (that is, if you live in reality), but there are absolute truths. Just because some say the sky is purple doesn't mean it is. There are absolute truths such as gravity, time, space and matter, to name a few.

Another absolute truth is God's word. Whatever God says comes to pass. For example, when God created the world, how did he do it? He simply spoke, *"'Let there be light'; and there was light"* (Genesis 1:3 NKJV) and:

'Let Us make man in Our image, according to Our likeness; let them have dominion over the fish of the sea, over the birds of the air, and over the cattle, over all the earth and over every creeping thing that creeps on the earth.' (Genesis 1:26 NKJV)

If you read the first chapter of Genesis, you'll see a definite pattern of God speaking and things becoming reality. If you're looking for solid absolute truth, look no further. God's word is recorded all throughout the pages of the Bible; and yes, the Bible was written by men, but all the men wrote under the influence of the Holy Spirit. *"For prophecy never had its origin in the human will, but prophets, though human, spoke from God as they were carried along by the Holy Spirit."* (2 Peter 1:21 NIV) 2 Timothy 3:16-17 (NIV) also says, *"All Scripture is God-breathed and is useful for teaching, rebuking, correcting and training in righteousness, so that the servant of God may be thoroughly equipped for every good work."* So, we know that the Bible is indeed God's word, and God's word is indeed absolute truth.

Let me share my stories now. Afterward, I will discuss some more on how God activates his power through faith in his word. The first testimony I would like to share is a financial one. I was going through a rather difficult time in my life, and had taken on some financial burdens I had not anticipated. They really weighed me down. I was single and had a mortgage, car payment, student loans, and credit cards; and paid out a lump sum for a recent divorce. It was taking its toll on me. But on the converse, I now had more free time per se to pray and read my Bible; and I started to really take my walk with Christ more seriously.

One thing that I read about in the Bible that was weighing on my mind was the concept of tithing. I had never really tried doing it, and was always too scared of what my wife would say if I gave 10% of our earnings to the church we attended. I wanted to try it now, but how in the world would I be able to do that with the financial situation I was in? I gave it some thought over several weeks, and decided I would start putting money into a separate account that would go to my church. I had 10% of my check direct-deposited into that account; and if I missed church for a week, I would still have that money in that account and could write a check when I attended. I had to be willing to trust God and let go of that money, and know that he would take care of all my needs.

This is the one area that God does ask you to test him on, so I did just that. Malachi 3:10 (NIV) says:

Bring the whole tithe into the storehouse, that there may be food in my house. TEST ME in this,' says the LORD Almighty, 'and see if I will not throw open the floodgates of heaven and pour out so much blessing that there will not be room enough to store it.

Even though I was strapped financially, I decided to go forward. That Sunday, I wrote a check for the money I had in the account and put it in the offering plate. I felt good about it, but still a little worried about my situation at home.

I didn't give it much thought again until I received a surprising letter in the mail about two weeks later. Remember how I said I was sponsored by a supplement company? They paid for my expenses when I traveled for them, and gave me a monthly supply of whatever supplements I wanted. They were even going to give me money each month; unfortunately, I had never seen any of that. I was completely happy with getting around $500 worth of supplements for free each month, so I never said anything.

Now, back to the letter in the mail. It was from IDS, the supplement company that I was sponsored by. This letter came literally two weeks after I started tithing, and you will never believe what was in it and what it said.

I was already a month late on my car payment that month, and that was weighing on my mind as I started to open the letter. I opened it up and pulled out a letter, and my eyes were instantly drawn to a check for $1,800. I had no idea what this check was for. I was overwhelmed because I now had money to make my car payment, but also pay off a few other bills and credit cards.

But what floored me the most was what the letter inside said. It was handwritten by Joe the owner of IDS. The letter explained that he had been busy and was finally catching up on accounting, and he had noticed they had not given me $200 a month like he said he was going to, and wanted to do just that. The check covered 9 months' worth of payments.

But I will never forget what Joe said in his letter at the very end: "I noticed that we had not given you the monthly stipend like we had promised, so here's money from heaven." Say what? Why in the world would he end the letter like that? "So here's money from heaven"??? Was this coincidence? He knew nothing of my financial status and my personal life at the time, so the only explanation was it was one of those God things. I was simply amazed; it was like God was saying, "Trust me, Shiloe, I always have your back."

To fast-forward this story, I continued to tithe for a period of over two years. I don't even remember how it happened or many of the details, but I found myself almost completely debt-free except for my mortgage. It is amazing how God works. I am not saying this will happen for everyone, but I am saying that if you trust God to provide for you, he will in some way and in some fashion. It is just our job to trust and let God activate his power by having faith in him.

The second testimony I want to share is just as amazing, and is also related to trusting in God's word. A few years back, I had two Doberman Pinschers named Roxie and Ozzie that were, like most pets, a part of the family. They were like my kids at the time, before I had kids, of course. This story is about my male Doberman, Ozzie. I started noticing Ozzie fall while running, for no reason at all. It started out as just a random thing, then became more concerning as the frequency of the falls increased. Then he started not to get up at all when I called him, so I became very concerned and decided to get him into the vet to see what the issue might be.

I was told by the vet it was probably just arthritis setting in, and he prescribed an anti-inflammatory medication to see if that helped. After a few weeks with no improvement, I decided to take him to another vet because he was getting worse instead of better. The vet performed a few X-rays, and concluded that the reason he was falling and unable to get up at certain times was because he more than likely had a mass or tumor in his spine. I could opt for surgery and have additional testing done, but I decided not to put him through all that because he was already around 9 years old. The life expectancy of a Doberman is around 10-12 years. It got worse as time went by, and it got to the point where I was physically picking him up and carrying him outside to go the bathroom. He just would not get up anymore.

I was deeply saddened because I knew the time had come to put him down, and there was no hope for him to get better. That night, I went to bed and prayed; and when I was praying, it came to mind how God had healed people in the Bible. Jesus healed many people, and his disciples did the same. If Jesus could heal people, why wouldn't he also be able to heal animals? A Bible verse, James 5:14-15 (NIV), became stuck in my head:

Is any among you sick? Let them call for the elders of the church to pray over them and anoint them with oil in the name of the Lord. And the prayer offered in faith will make the sick person well; the Lord will raise them up.

I figured, why not? I will pray over Ozzie. After all, what do I have to lose? I went online and printed out a bunch of healing scriptures, and got some oil as well. I said a prayer, then put the oil on Ozzie and laid my hands on him; and went through the list of healing scriptures three times. I then went to bed for the night.

I woke up the next morning not expecting anything to be different. But when I came downstairs, to my amazement, he was standing and looking up at me. I rushed down and gave him a hug and wondered: *Did God do this?* I was looking at a completely different dog. I went to work that morning and rushed home afterward, and found him walking like he normally did. That night, I prayed over him again and went to bed.

I soon realized that he was completely healed. It was instantaneous! There simply was no other explanation. I told my friends at work, and my best friend Steve said it was just the medication finally kicking in. I then explained to him that Ozzie had stopped taking his medication weeks ago, and there is only one explanation for his healing. Could this be coincidence again? I think not; in fact, I am certain.

Ozzie went on to live another 4 years, and he ran and played like nothing had ever happened to him. It was amazing that a dog who could not even stand and had to be physically carried in and out to use the restroom was now able to run at full speed. It was simply mind-blowing!

God's word is true, and he does answer prayers and perform miracles. He can do amazing things because his word is truth, and absolute truth at that. I am not saying he will answer every prayer in the manner or style in which he did in the two prior testimonies, but I am saying with faith that you will be amazed by what God can do. I truly believe that in both cases, it was faith that activated God's power. I had faith in his word and acted on that faith, and God did the rest.

All throughout the Bible, we see that it is faith that activates God's power. Abraham was justified by faith; and he didn't just believe God, he acted on his faith as proof. Noah acted on his faith and built an ark, and saved himself and his family from the great flood. Moses, by faith, acted and led the Israelites out of Egyptian captivity. During Jesus' time, people were healed by faith, and many miracles were performed by faith.

There were also a few times when Jesus could not do miracles because of lack of faith. An example is in Mark 6:5 (NLT): *"And because of their unbelief, he couldn't do any miracles among them except to place his hands on a few sick people and heal them."* As you can see, one common requirement needed to unlock God's power is faith. God's desire is for all people to be saved and have eternal life as well, but it is faith in Jesus that provides that saving grace. To unlock God's amazing power, we must have genuine faith in him. Only then will you see amazing things happen.

Children are a gift from the Lord; they are a reward from him.

— *Psalm 127:3 (NLT)*

CHAPTER #7

Expecting but Unexpected:
The Birthday Gift of a Lifetime

I have received some awesome birthday gifts over my 47 years of life, but there is one that stands out miles above all the rest. I could have never imagined in a million years the gift I would receive on February 27th, 2011.

First, here's a little backdrop to the story I am about to share so you can understand why this was the best birthday gift ever, even though some of life's biggest trials soon followed. It was January of 2011. My wife and I were expecting twins in June, and were both excited to have kids for the first time. We were doing the normal maternity visits and getting ultrasounds on schedule. The doctors had determined that my wife was high-risk because she carried twins, and referred her to a specialist down in Columbus. She was also placed on bed rest as a precautionary measure.

Some complications soon followed, and she was transferred down to Ohio State for tests and observation. It was February 26th, and it appeared we would be spending my birthday at the hospital, as an overnight stay was certain and an extended stay was in the plans. If she were to give birth at this point, the twins would be approximately three months early, and would have a very little chance of survival. She would remain on bed rest and observation indefinitely. The goal was to hold the twins in utero for as long as possible to improve their chances of survival in case of premature birth. She was in her hospital bed, and I had a small pullout bed in the same room; and we headed to bed for the night. What would happen next would change both our lives forever.

It was about 1:30 am on February 27th. She had woken up to use the restroom, and that was when I heard her call out in a panicked voice. As she came out of the restroom, all I remember is seeing a tiny head poking out; and panic ensued.

We immediately called for the nurses, and that was when chaos soon took over the entire room. A medical team had rushed into the room, and it appeared that a delivery was going to take place unexpectedly. There were staff members rushing around, and a neonatal team was summoned and waiting right outside the room within minutes. At this point, I was deeply saddened because I remembered what the doctors had told us, and that the twins' chance of survival was minimal.

The OB-GYN was going to deliver the baby whether anyone was ready or not. Everything was happening so fast, it was hard to recall every detail in the mass chaos. I do remember that Kellen was completely out now, and passed without hesitation over to the neonatal team. The neonatologist began the tedious process of trying to intubate Kellen. He was obviously way too premature to breathe on his own as his lungs were immensely underdeveloped. I recall the neonatologist trying multiple times to get a tube small enough into his lungs, and finally I heard him call a time. The team left the area, and they took Kellen away. Reis was still in utero, and they were attending to mom now.

I had assumed that Kellen was deceased, and it was not until about 20 minutes later that I learned he was alive and under the care of the neonatal team. Luckily, we were at a level-three neonatal intensive care unit (NICU) at the Ohio State University, and they were equipped for this situation. Otherwise, there would be have been no chance of survival at all. Never would I have imagined a birthday like this in a million years.

Reis remained in utero for another four days before he had to be taken by Caesarean section due to complications, and was born on March 3rd. They were born approximately 3 months early, with a combined weight of 2.9 lbs. Kellen weighed a mere 1.1 lbs, while Reis weighed 1.8 lbs. Both had survived the birth process, but the journey had just begun; and I was now a father of twin boys fighting for their very lives.

Over the next few weeks, there were many obstacles to overcome for both boys, and we were at the beginning of a long NICU stay of several months. Both boys were in specially designed enclosures to protect them from infection, and protect their fragile and super-thin skin. They described how it would feel for the boys if anyone just touched their skin at this gestational age. Because their skin was so thin, whenever someone would touch them, the touched area would feel like it was burning.

A few days went by before the first major event happened. Kellen soon developed sepsis, and was now critically ill. I remember the call I received that night as if it were yesterday. The call came in at 3 am, and it was the nurse from the NICU. She advised me that we should come in to see Kellen because it did not look good, and they did not think he would make it much longer and we might want to say our goodbyes.

I prayed as I did every single day, and I kept praying in my head as we drove into the hospital. We were very fortunate as we had a ton of people praying for Kellen and Reis through the whole process: people we did not even know, as well as people from various churches. With the use of social media, I had set up a page on Facebook for the boys and kept people up to date with their progress, and I know prayer chains were generated for them through that media outlet. Needless to say, there were many voices being lifted to heaven to pray for Kellen and Reis.

We arrived at the hospital and walked into a horrific scene. Kellen was being manually bagged by the doctor. It was a scene that will be etched into my brain forever. His life was literally in the hands of a special neonatologist we only saw two times the entire time the boys were at Ohio State, and later at Nationwide Children's Hospital in Columbus. After many hours and special care, Kellen made it through that episode. It was a miracle from God that he survived that night.

Days passed before we found out both boys had patent ductus arteriosus (PDA), which is a persistent opening between the two major blood vessels leading from the heart. The opening, called the ductus arteriosus, is a normal part of a baby's circulatory system that closes shortly after birth.[2] Theirs did not close, so they were transferred at this point from Ohio State to Nationwide Children's Hospital for the delicate surgery.

At the time, there was only one surgeon from Pennsylvania who would come to Children's to perform this surgery on an as-needed basis. This is also a risky type of surgery because if the surgeon makes one small wrong move, the possibility of bleeding out is almost certain. They successfully had the surgery, but the boys needed another surgery for their eyes soon after. This was to save their eyesight, which was also from being born so prematurely. Once again, the staff at Children's Hospital successfully completed that surgery.

---

2 "Patent ductus arteriosus (PDA)". Mayo Clinic website. Mayo Foundation for Medical Education and Research, 2019, https://www.mayoclinic.org/diseases-conditions/patent-ductus-arteriosus/symptoms-causes/syc-20376145

Things seemed to be getting better. Then they took a turn for the worse. Kellen started to develop an infection, and his breathing became horrible. Even while on a ventilator, his oxygen levels declined. He was at the worst point possible, and had maxed out on oxygen and nitrous oxide and was building up carbon monoxide at an alarming rate.

Seemingly out of nowhere, that same neonatologist that saved Kellen at Ohio State showed up (but this time, at Children's) and began giving orders to try to reverse the dangerous gas levels in Kellen's body. He was switched over to an oscillating ventilator, which basically kept his lungs open but violently shook his entire body the entire time he was hooked up to it. By God's grace, Kellen made it through that episode; and eventually recovered.

I still wonder to this day: Was that doctor sent by God? Who was he, and why did we only see him at the two worst times in Kellen's short life? Reis had his bad times as well, but they all paled in comparison to what Kellen endured. But God was protecting both of them. I won't go into more details about the remaining months at the hospital, but there are many more stories I could tell, and miracles I could share. There are many stories from the years after they came home as well; but through it all, God was right there, protecting their lives the entire time. The point I wanted to make is that the power of prayer sustained both my boys. God showed up because of the prayers and faith of many people.

Every life is precious in the eyes of God; and every person has a purpose in life, no matter if they are premature, disabled, deformed, or unwanted. We know this from God's word when speaking to the prophet Jeremiah: *"I knew you before I formed you in your mother's womb. Before you were born I set you apart and appointed you as my prophet to the nations."* (Jeremiah 1:5 NLT) Job 31:15 (ESV) also states: *"Did not he who made me in the womb make him? And did he not one fashion us in the womb?"* You see, God knows each one of us from even before we were conceived and until the day he calls us home. Even when a child is born with disabilities, the Lord has plans for that child and is useful in the eyes of God.

Jeremiah 29:11 (NIV) gives us another reminder of this: *"For I know the plans I have for you," declares the Lord, "plans to prosper you and not to harm you, plans to give you hope and a future."* All life is sacred and has value, and the creator of all life knows us personally and has plans for our lives. I can't imagine life now without my sons. I thank God every day for the gift of being a father, and for the joy that they bring me each day.

Unfortunately, we live in a society where life is not valued. Many people do not see the unborn as people. We have no place for the elderly, and discount them if they are not productive members of society. I know that at the time my sons were born, they could have legally been terminated in all 50 states. But look at them now: they are amazing little people with a God-given purpose and destiny. Any parent would agree that children are truly a gift from God above, and one of the greatest gifts to us outside of grace and salvation.

Psalm 127:3 (ESV) says: *"Behold, children are a heritage from the Lord, the fruit of the womb a reward."* Children and family are something we should cherish and not take for granted; the family is the very fabric that knits us together and brings much joy. Never take a day for granted with your family because as we know, this life is short, and we are never promised tomorrow. Therefore, we should enjoy every day we have with them.

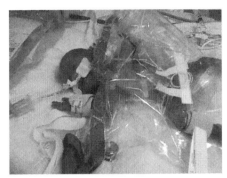 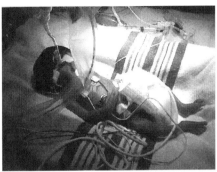

Reis born March 3rd 2011 at 1lb 8oz, this picture was taken just after c-section delivery

Kellen born on February 27th 2011 at 1lb 1oz., he was the size of my palm

Kellen and Reis 6 years after birth

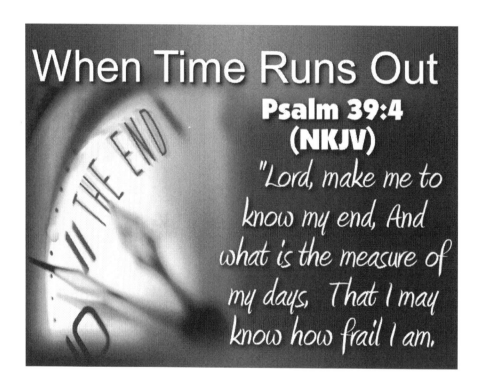

CHAPTER #8

When Time Runs Out

One day, you will wake up and there won't be any more time to do the things you've always wanted. Do it now.

— Paulo Coelho

As I mentioned in an earlier chapter, none of us knows the time, date, or place we will take our last breath. Nobody, no matter how rich, smart, attractive, famous, or powerful, can escape the reality of death. Our time is limited; and at some point, we will all give an account of our lives. Some of us will awaken from death in joy and be in the presence of our creator; and others, to face the most terrifying news and fate anyone could ever imagine. We will all stand before the throne and judgment seat of the creator of the universe.

If you are lucky, you may get 100 years on earth. But for the most part, that doesn't happen to a lot of us. We have a select number of years to get right before God, and get to know the one who made us. We can choose to seek God and fulfill his will for our lives, or we can continue in rebellion and seek our own will and purposely forsake the God who created us. Are you seeking God in your life; or are you living each day like there is no tomorrow, only seeking pleasure and the things of this world? Are you living like your time is unlimited, and waiting for a later time to follow God's will in your life? Something to think about, for sure!

I would like to share a story of a very special friend of mine. We no longer work together because I had moved, and he later passed away. But for years, we worked together, trained in the gym together, shot guns together, and shared stories together. He was not only a best friend to me; he was like a brother. I would describe him as very passionate, as well as a little rough around the edges. He was the kind of guy who would do anything for you and help you out whenever needed. But as I mentioned, he was also little rough around the edges and would swear like a sailor. He was tatted up and had full sleeves, as they call it in the tattoo world. If you saw the guy on the street, you would think he was a Mexican drug cartel member. Like they always say, you cannot judge a book by its cover. He was a professional with several degrees, and a very intelligent healthcare professional who did a lot of reading.

When he did something, he did it to the max, holding nothing back. He was truly a unique guy. But he always came across as missing something when we would talk at lunch. He was missing that piece that God puts in all of us: that need for a relationship with him. He would ask many questions, and was certainly seeking God. He still swore a lot and with his intense demeanor, his blood pressure would often be out of control. I would tell him he needs to get it under control; and jokingly, he would gasp for air and act as if he were having a heart attack.

I believe he was seeking his true passion, and I know he was extremely dissatisfied with his job as a pharmacist. He eventually decided to find his true passion as far as career goes. He left pharmacy and pursued a career in law enforcement, and finally found his career. It was great to see him happy, and complete his training and officially become a deputy for the Franklin County sheriff's department.

I will never forget the call I received on September 1st, 2016. I remember picking up the phone, and hearing these words come from the other end of the line: "He is gone."

I remember saying "What do you mean?" in disbelief.

"He died this morning when doing a drill for training for the sheriff's department. He fell down, and they could not revive him."

My best friend had just died of a massive heart attack at the age of 46. He seemed to have everything going for him and was finally in a career he loved, and had recently married. BAM! Just like that, it was all over.

After the reality set in and the funeral was over, I reminisced about all the times we shared and the talks we had at lunch about faith and Jesus and what life is all about. I started wondering to myself: Did he truly know Jesus? Was he saved? These are questions only God knows the answers to, for only God knows his heart. I know he still had a lot of questions and doubts about a lot of things concerning faith. It really bothered me because I didn't want to think he died not knowing the grace that Jesus brings through faith.

His death was a turning point in my life. After his passing, things started to change in my personal life as far as work schedule, kids, and finances went. So I felt God's timing was right for me to pursue the calling he had placed in my heart many years prior. I decided to enroll in graduate school to pursue a degree in Theology so I could be better equipped to fulfill my calling.

I didn't want another close friend (or anyone, for that matter) to die unexpectedly without knowing the saving power of Jesus Christ. I felt my calling was to share the Gospel in whatever way God leads me. To do that, I must first be equipped to give an account for the faith that I hold. I kept thinking about one of the last things Jesus said when he was with us on earth and how he gave us the "Great Commission". In Matthew 28:16-20 (NKJV), Jesus is talking with his disciples before he was arrested and eventually crucified:

Then the eleven disciples went away to Galilee, to the mountain which Jesus had appointed for them. When they saw Him, they worshiped Him; but some doubted.

And Jesus came and spoke to them, saying, 'All authority has been given to Me in heaven and on earth. Go therefore and make disciples of all nations, baptizing them in the name of the Father and of the Son and of the Holy Spirit, teaching them to observe all things that I have commanded you; and lo, I am with you always, even to the end of the age.' Amen.

Unfortunately, I will not have another opportunity to talk with my friend and give him the assurance that he was looking for, and I will not know until I reach heaven if he was truly saved or not. In his case, because it was an unexpected heart attack, he didn't get a second chance to decide to follow Jesus if he had not already; and his fate was sealed the moment he took his last breath. It reminds me of another quote, and something to think about: "Eternity is one breath away."

Others are more fortunate, and go through something traumatic and live to tell the story—like I did when I had my motorcycle accident. My father had a similar experience; and his is a story of God's grace, and another chance to make changes in his life. A few years prior to his bypass surgery, he had a mild stroke and went to the emergency room. After testing and various evaluations, it was discovered that both of his carotid arteries were completely blocked; and he was receiving blood flow to his brain through periphery arteries on the back of his neck. Most people will never have both their carotids completely blocked because they will die from a major stroke before that ever happens. He was lucky, and got another chance to make some lifestyle changes.

A few years later, after having an annual stress test, it was again discovered that he had some blockages in his main heart valves; and would need surgery immediately due to the extent and location of those blockages. Stents were not possible because of the location of the blockage, and a triple bypass was eminent.

Bypass surgery is no laughing matter or walk in the park because they stop the heart completely and pump your blood through a machine that places oxygen into the blood. This is because the lungs are also shut down. The blood is then reintroduced into the body after it is oxygenated. Because of the blockage already in his carotids, this procedure would be even more risky; and the chances of a major stroke occurring during the procedure itself increased tremendously.

He had a surgery date scheduled in Toledo, Ohio, but it did not sit right with the entire family. To make a long story short, by a sheer miracle and working of God, he could get into the Cleveland Clinic at the last minute with one of the best cardiac surgeons in the world. I remember when he went in for surgery; I thought it could possibly be the last time I would see him, so we said prayers over him for protection and saw him off to surgery. They gave us an idea of how long the surgery would take, so we were expecting to wait about 2.5 hours once the major portion of the surgery had begun. We then headed down to the cafeteria to get a bite to eat.

I then got a page to come back to the reception desk. I rushed back, and was told the doctor wanted to see us up on a different floor. This all transpired 45 minutes into the surgery; so I was worried that they had indeed run into some complications, as they mentioned this was quite possible. Our anxiety arose as we were certain the surgery could not be done at this point.

We all gathered in a private room on the fourth floor, and waited for the arrival of the doctor. Tension was high at this point, and my mom had feared the worst. As the doctor entered the room, she began to cry. The doctor came in and looked at us with a peculiar stare. It was almost as he was saying with his look on his face, "Oh no, who died?" The next words he said were, in fact, completely different than what everyone was expecting. He said, "Well, it is over; and the surgery went well."

Everyone sighed in relief, and my mom immediately ran up to the surgeon and gave him a big hug. My dad would be okay and will recover to live another day. He is one of the lucky ones who not only got a second chance, but a third one as well. Not all of us are that lucky; and sometimes, it is without warning, such as in my best friend's case.

The point I wanted to drill home here is that there is never a better time than now to make changes in your life and start living for God now. You are never promised tomorrow, and no one knows when they will take their last breath. Instead of waiting for a better time to follow the Lord or a better circumstance, why not start now? Start while you still have time and still can share the Gospel with those you love. It doesn't matter how old or young you are; God can still use you to reach others. Some of us are just beginning their journey in faith, while others have been walking with the Lord for years. But in each case, God is able to use you and make an impact on the ones around you. I encourage you to start now if you have not, and begin to learn what God has in store for your life.

This reminds me of an adage that correlates with living a healthy lifestyle. The best time you can start taking care of your health and body is twenty years ago; the second-best time is now! This same principle applies to your faith and walk as a Christian. It doesn't matter whether you have been walking with Jesus for years or not. If not years ago, the next-best time to start is now.

The easiest way to start is to say the sinner's prayer and ask Jesus to start working in your life and to fill you with his Holy Spirit. Start by praying this:

Father, I know that I have broken your laws and my sins have separated me from you. I am truly sorry, and now I want to turn away from my past sinful life toward you. Please forgive me, and help me avoid sinning again. I believe that your son, Jesus Christ died for my sins, was resurrected from the dead, is alive, and hears my prayer. I invite Jesus to become the Lord of my life, to rule and reign in my heart from this day forward. Please send your Holy Spirit to help me obey You, and to do Your will for the rest of my life. In Jesus' name I pray, Amen.[3]

3"Sinner's Prayer". AllAboutGod.com, https://www.allaboutgod.com/sinners-prayer.htm.

CHAPTER #9

Trick or Treat?

The greatest trick the Devil ever pulled was convincing the world he didn't exist.

— *Roger Kint, The Usual Suspects, 1995*

Hopefully, you are beginning to see some of the truths of God's word; and how they apply to your life and the situations we all may face. I hope you also are starting to think about your future in eternity, and what might come after your time is up here on earth.

I wanted to share with you some of my life stories, and how they have made me see things from a different perspective: a view that has eternity in mind, and how God has given us all the choice to accept his grace and will for our lives, or the choice to live a life separate from him and all eternity. Remember, God is a fair and just God; he will never force you to follow his will. He may call you, but you still can reject him. (There is a whole theological debate on predestination, but we won't dive into that here.) If you decide to live separate from God, he will give you exactly what you want for all eternity. I hope that is not the decision you'll make, but it's something I want you to think about.

One of the difficult things we'll face, if we do decide to seek God's will for our lives and follow Jesus, is the constant attacks by the devil along the way. You may even find the attacks of the enemy worse as you move closer to God. But knowing God's word is one of the best ways to defend yourself against those attacks. If you're a new

Christian or have been one for years, it is vital that you read and study the Bible. It is an instruction book for life and every situation. It is also the way God speaks to us. His inspired word is a gift to us. Just like working out, reading the Bible builds our spiritual muscle and helps us get stronger in faith.

We must be willing to use the tools God gives us to defend ourselves against Satan and his schemes. Paul, writing to the Ephesians, gives us some great tools:

Finally, be strong in the Lord and in his mighty power. Put on the full armor of God, so that you can take your stand against the devil's schemes. For our struggle is not against flesh and blood, but against the rulers, against the authorities, against the powers of this dark world and against the spiritual forces of evil in the heavenly realms. Therefore put on the full armor of God, so that when the day of evil comes, you may be able to stand your ground, and after you have done everything, to stand. Stand firm then, with the belt of truth buckled around your waist, with the breastplate of righteousness in place, and with your feet fitted with the readiness that comes from the gospel of peace. In addition to all this, take up the shield of faith, with which you can extinguish all the flaming arrows of the evil one. Take the helmet of salvation and the sword of the Spirit, which is the word of God. (Ephesians 6:10-17 NIV)

As you can see, Paul is describing what the Roman legionaries used as their armor in his day, and was comparing it to what we can use against Satan. Most of the armor is for defensive purposes only, except for the sword of the spirit, which is an offensive weapon. We will see how Jesus used that in a moment. I encourage you to try to set aside time each day to study and read from God's word. This will help you tremendously when facing some of the tricks the devil uses on us.

If we successfully deflect the devil, we will experience the treat per se that God has for us.

The reason I titled the chapter "Trick or Treat?" is because it is such a familiar term to everyone, and I like the analogy when thinking of our spiritual lives. Do we want to be tricked or to experience the treat of God's truth? After all, no one really wants a trick; isn't a treat always better to receive? Knowing the various tricks Satan uses will help us defend ourselves better against his tactics. Since the dawn of time, Satan has used the same old tricks and isn't all that creative when trying to tempt us. Although he has many ways of making us falter, he has three big tricks that he typically uses. 1 John 2:16 (NIV) says: *"For everything in the world—the lust of the flesh, the lust of the eyes, and the pride of life—comes not from the Father but from the world."*

Satan started out in the Garden of Eden, where he tempted Eve; and he first used these three methods to bring about the fall of all mankind. Then later, he tempted Jesus with these three same methods. The first temptation was after Jesus had been fasting for 40 days. Satan appealed to the lust of the flesh by tempting Jesus to convert some stones into bread so he could satisfy his hunger. The next temptation concerns the lust of the eyes as Satan showed him all the kingdoms of the world; and offered immediate Messiahship without having to suffer on the cross, which is the very reason for why he came to earth. All Jesus had to do was bow down and worship Satan. Lastly, he told Jesus to basically jump off a cliff so God's angels would save him. This temptation concerns the pride of life and tries to get Jesus to abuse his own powers, as well as put God's word into question.

Each time, Jesus was able to fend off these temptations by the very word of God (sword of the spirit). Jesus knew scripture very well, and used the very words of God to put Satan back in his place and conquer each temptation. We have this same ability and power to overcome Satan if we take the time to know and use the word of God. Sadly, very few of us read or study the Bible today, so we have little to no knowledge regarding the power that God's word holds.

I encourage you to spend time reading and studying God's word to equip yourself with the knowledge it contains to successfully fend off the devil's attacks. You will certainly find the answers for almost every problem or circumstance that you run into every day. Don't fall victim to the attacks of Satan and fall into despair, depression, or hopelessness! You have more power than you think! After all, the spirit of the almighty lives inside you when you follow Jesus; you can do all things and overcome all things. Just remember this powerful scripture when tempted or persecuted: *"I can do all things through Christ who strengthens me."* (Philippians 4:13 NKJV)

The Bible is such a powerful resource for life because it is the inspired word of God. I find it almost unbelievable how many self-professed Christians never pick up the Bible or spend any time at all studying the word of God. Because I come from a fitness background, I have people asking me all the time for tips on losing weight or gaining muscle, or tips on eating healthy or exercising to improve their overall health. When I respond with the two greatest things they can do, exercise and eating right, they never like that answer. The same holds true when building up your faith: the two best things you can do are pray and read your Bible. People want a quick fix that requires little or no effort on their part. Eating right, exercising, praying, and reading the Bible are too much work for many. We live in a world of instant gratification, and it is uncomfortable to work hard for some things. It is almost laughable, and I will tell you why in a bit. Remember, the only real excuse you have is the one you make!

I want to expand a bit on this concept of reading your Bible. When I ask people why they don't read their Bible, I get one of two different excuses. Either they don't understand it, or… Can you take a wild guess? If you guessed that they just don't have time, you nailed it. As I just said, the only excuse you really have is the one you make. The sad truth is that it is just not a priority for them, similar to those not living a healthy lifestyle. With all the readily available resources out there such as Bible lessons, podcasts, and many others, the excuse of not understanding the Bible starts to crumble fast. The excuse, "I don't have time", is because you're not setting time side; and again, it is just not a priority to you.

Not living a healthy lifestyle or reading your Bible because of lack of time is a horrible excuse when you start to budget your time and see where it goes. Start making a log for a week, and you will soon see you do have the time; it's just spent on what you value more. It amazes me how many people have told me they don't have time to do these things; then literally five minutes later, I will hear them in conversation talking about the latest episode of *American Idol* or something similar. They can literally talk for hours about the latest and greatest TV shows, but can't tell you anything that is in the Bible.

How many hours do you waste every week watching TV or scrolling through social media posts? According to a Nielsen report, the average American adult watches five hours and four minutes of television a day! That's an average of 35.5 hours a week![4][5] And of

---

4 John Koblin, "How Much Do We Love TV? Let Us Count the Ways". June 30, 2016, *The New York Times*, https://www.nytimes.com/2016/07/01/business/media/nielsen-survey-media-viewing.html.

5 David Hinckley, "Average American watches 5 hours of TV per day, report shows". March 5, 2014, *New York Daily News*, https://www.nydailynews.com/life-style/average-american-watches-5-hours-tv-day-article-1.1711954.

course, older people watch even more than that. You can see that the excuse of lack of time just doesn't add up to a hill of beans.

I urge you to really take inventory of your time and priorities. Is following Jesus and equipping yourself with God's word a priority, or is watching countless hours of television more important? Your eternal destiny depends on your decision. Not only that, but you will be better equipped to face any situation that life throws at you with confidence and the truth of God's word. Just like Jesus was able to fend off Satan's attacks, you too will be able to fight off any attacks because you will be fully equipped with the armor of God.

CHAPTER #10

. . . .

It's All Meaningless

Life without GOD no matter how seemingly
valuable leads to emptiness.[6]

You're probably wondering why the chapter is titled "It's All Meaningless". What in the world do I mean by that? The Book of Ecclesiastes is one of my favorite books in the Old Testament because I truly enjoy the wisdom of God. He has given us a few books of wisdom in the Old Testament, and Ecclesiastes is one of them. It is full of so many truths and points that really make you ponder the meaning of life and what it is all about. In fact, Ecclesiastes deals with exactly that: what life is all about.

We don't know for certain who wrote the Book of Ecclesiastes, but scholars are mostly certain it was written by Solomon, the wisest person to ever live in human history. Throughout the book, Solomon used the word "Hevel" 38 times when he described the meaning of life. So, what exactly does "Hevel" mean? It is a Hebrew word that has many translations, depending on the version of the Bible that you have. But its meaning is essentially the same. Most commonly, you will see "vanity" or "meaningless" in most translations, but maybe a better translation is "smoke" or "vapor". Another good translation is breath that is already spent—so essentially, a "waste of breath". No matter what translation you go with, the idea that Solomon was trying

6www.Awesomequotes4u.com

to convey is something that is fleeting or visible for a moment, then gone and out of grasp.

He describes all we do in life as Hevel; and if you just read the Book of Ecclesiastes without understanding the full context, it can be very depressing and hopeless. Solomon had everything he ever wanted in life, and had it to the max. Women, money, power, fame, material things, and whatever he could think of, he had it. But in all this, he still was not completely happy or satisfied. In his old age, through wisdom, he discovered that true happiness and purpose is doing what you were created to do by your creator. The money, power, fame, women, and earthly things are "Hevel" or pointless, meaningless, vanity... You get the idea.

So, what was his conclusion regarding life? What brings true happiness and fulfillment? Solomon ends the book by saying:

Now all has been heard; here is the conclusion of the matter: Fear God and keep his commandments, for this is the duty of all mankind. For God will bring every deed into judgment, including every hidden thing, whether it is good or evil. (Ecclesiastes 12:13-14 NIV)

We will all face judgment someday before an almighty and Holy God; so in whatever we do, we should seek God and follow his lead for our lives. Later, we will show you how keeping God's commandments truly does bring happiness and content hearts. We can only find true happiness and lasting satisfaction by doing what we were created to do, and giving thanks and worship to a creator who genuinely deserves our praise and worship. We will also see that by fearing the Lord and keeping his commandments, we are protected from all sorts of dangers and evils. God's commandments are designed to protect us because he truly loves us and cares for our well-being.

In summary, we waste a lot of time, money, and life pursuing things that will not bring us true joy and happiness. In the end, it is all Hevel. Seeking God and following his plan and will for our lives are what bring true and lasting joy and peace in our lives. We should reframe our mindset and keep our eyes focused on the one who made us, and seek his purpose in our lives. Only then we will have true and lasting satisfaction in life.

We have discovered that most of everything we pursue in life is meaningless if we do not have eternity in mind. Everything will eventually be a memory in the halls of time. This life and its pursuits are a fleeting moment in time in comparison to eternity. I encourage you to think about your eternal destiny, and whether you are saved. A question I want to ask you and think about is are you really saved?

God is the author and source of all life; and without God, we have no life. Sin has separated us from God, and thus separated us from the source of life. That is why we live maybe a hundred years (if we are lucky), then die. We were not originally created to die, but rather live forever in the garden that God had created for us. The real concern isn't with dying a physical death; what comes after that is what we should be worried about. There is a second death that is far worse than dying physically, and that is spiritual death or eternal separation from God.

You may ask this question: Why do we need salvation, anyway? Great question. The Bible tells us that because we have sinned against God, we are spiritually dead. Ephesians 2:1 (NIV) reads: *"As for you, you were dead in your transgressions and sins."* None of us are exempt from this either, as we read in Romans 3:23 (NIV): *"for all have sinned and fall short of the glory of God."* We are all in the same boat. Not one of us are free from sin; and because of this, we all deserve eternal separation from God and eternal death.

Fortunately, we do have a savior and thus, salvation. I am not going to go into the details and teaching of Hebrews 9 in scripture; but it teaches that without the shedding of blood, there is no remission of sins. In the Old Testament, they routinely had to sacrifice animals for the atonement of sins. But today, we have Jesus, who shed his blood on the cross for us. He is the perfect sacrifice for one and for all. God, in his infinite mercy, knew we were not able to save ourselves, and knew we could not pay the price for our salvation. Because of this fact, he became man and lived among us and paid that price for us.

So back to the million-dollar question: Are you saved? To first answer that, you must know how you are saved, and Nicodemus asked Jesus that very question. Nicodemus was a very prominent Jewish Pharisee at the time when Jesus walked the earth; and in John 3:3-6 (NIV), he plainly asked him how to enter the kingdom of God:

Jesus replied, 'Very truly I tell you, no one can see the kingdom of God unless they are born again.'

How can someone be born when they are old?' Nicodemus asked. 'Surely they cannot enter a second time into their mother's womb to be born!'

Jesus answered, 'Very truly I tell you, no one can enter the kingdom of God unless they are born of water and the Spirit. Flesh gives birth to flesh, but the Spirit gives birth to spirit.

Clearly, we must be born again to be saved. Jesus tells us that to be born again, we must be born of the spirit or "from above". But how in the world are we born from above? It is a difficult question to answer, but it is also rather simple. We need to genuinely seek God, and ask God to forgive us; and then do all we can to follow Jesus. We literally take up our cross and follow him.

Remember the sinner's prayer we covered at the end of Chapter 8? If you need to, go back and say that prayer again. God will then come into your heart and start to change your life, and shape you into a new person and transform you into the image of his son.

Again, I will ask you a challenging question: Are you saved? Jesus also told us that you can judge a tree by the fruit it bears. You must ask yourself: Are you bearing the fruit of the spirit? *"But the fruit of the Spirit is love, joy, peace, forbearance, kindness, goodness, faithfulness, gentleness and self-control."* (Galatians 5:22-23 NIV) I could go into more detail on each of these, but I encourage you to study them for yourself to see if you exemplify these things. Are you bearing the fruit of the Spirit?

Sadly, there are many people who go through life believing they are saved, or believing they are a "good" person and that God will surely have a place in heaven for them. This is a great deception of Satan himself. As we now know, we cannot save ourselves and need a savior. We are born again through faith in and of the works of Jesus. We are genuinely saved and born again if we continue in faith and start to produce the fruit of the spirit in our lives reflecting the image of Jesus to others.

Jesus clearly warns us that not all who profess to be his followers are true followers, as we read in Matthew 7:21-23 (NIV):

Not everyone who says to me, 'Lord, Lord,' will enter the kingdom of heaven, but the one who does the will of my Father who is in heaven. Many will say to me on that day, 'Lord, Lord, did we not prophesy in your name and in your name drive out demons and in your name perform many miracles?' Then I will tell them plainly, 'I never knew you. Away from me, you evildoers!'

Don't be one of those who ends up only deceiving yourself. We know many will profess to be followers of Christ; but, in fact, they've never known him. This is a good time to self-examine your own life, and the way you live and treat others. Are you bearing fruit and living a life that reflects that? Are you working daily to follow Jesus, reading God's word, and equipping yourself to fight off Satan's attacks? The question you must answer and only you can answer is: Are you born again?

Conclusion

I hope you enjoyed reading of some of my life stories and seeing how God has worked in my life, and how I have learned some valuable truths about life in general and how God's truth can be seen amid of all our life experiences. I also hope that by reading this book, you start to think about your own life and see how God has been involved all along; and really start think about your eternal destiny and what your purpose in life is. Maybe you have been a follower of Jesus for many years and just enjoy reading some good stories. Maybe you need to recharge your walk with the Lord. Or maybe you will share this book with someone who does not know the Lord, and it will inspire them to think about what lies ahead in their eternal destination. Whatever the situation or wherever you are in life, I hope this book was of benefit to you. After all, in the end, it is all about Jesus and all about where we will spend eternity.

The Bible is either true or it isn't. But I believe there is enough evidence logically and historically to know for certain that it is true and indeed God's inspired word to us all. For those who do not believe, what do you have to lose? If the Bible is not true, you will eventually die and that is the end forever. But if it is true, it has eternal consequences that will affect you, whether you like it or not. Why not see for yourself the difference that following Jesus will have in your life, and the true joy and peace you will experience?

I pray you seek God while there is still time. If you have already accepted Jesus as your personal Lord and savior, I pray you continue to live in peace and joy; and patiently wait for the day we will see him face to face. After all, the choice is ultimately yours. ETERNITY AWAITS.

Thank You

Thank you for taking the time to read about my personal journey so far in life toward eternity. Although following Jesus is a process and we will continue to struggle each day in that journey, God gives us the power to grow in faith. The more we stay on the narrow path and build ourselves up with the word of God, the stronger we become.

If you enjoyed this book and know someone who may benefit from it, please share it with them. If you would like to contact me and leave feedback, I can be reached at shiloesteinmetz@yahoo.com. Also, please leave a positive book review on Amazon so others may read it as well. A positive book review helps promote *Eternity Awaits* so others can start to think about their eternal future as well.

21 Day Bible Reading Challenge

They say if you do anything consistently for 21 days or more it becomes a habit. If you are following Jesus or have just begun your journey it is imperative that you equip yourself with the word of God. This not only strengthens your faith but also gives you power against the attacks of the Devil. I challenge you for the next 21 days to set 30 minutes a day a side to start equipping yourself with the word of God. We will start out with the Gospel of John for simplicity as there are 21 chapters and will allow for an easy reading of one chapter a day. I also encourage you to write some notes in the space available below each page. Just write down whatever comes to mind or maybe even try to summarize the main point of the chapter. By doing this you will have begun the process of serious Bible study. If you complete this challenge you will see that it is possible to stay in God's word daily and it will become a normal daily habit for you. Good Luck!

DAY ONE
Reading: JOHN CHAPTER 1

NOTES:

DAY TWO
Reading: JOHN CHAPTER 2

NOTES:

DAY THREE
Reading: JOHN CHAPTER 3

NOTES:

DAY FOUR
Reading: JOHN CHAPTER 4

NOTES:

DAY FIVE
Reading: JOHN CHAPTER 5

NOTES:

DAY SIX
Reading: JOHN CHAPTER 6

NOTES:

DAY SEVEN
Reading: JOHN CHAPTER 7

NOTES:

DAY EIGHT
Reading: JOHN CHAPTER 8

NOTES:

DAY NINE
Reading: JOHN CHAPTER 9

NOTES:

DAY TEN
Reading: JOHN CHAPTER 10

NOTES:

DAY ELEVEN
Reading: JOHN CHAPTER 11

NOTES:

DAY TWELVE
Reading: JOHN CHAPTER 12

NOTES:

DAY THIRTEEN
Reading: JOHN CHAPTER 13

NOTES:

DAY FOURTEEN
Reading: JOHN CHAPTER 14

NOTES:

DAY FIFTEEN
Reading: JOHN CHAPTER 15

NOTES:

DAY SIXTEEN
Reading: JOHN CHAPTER 16

NOTES:

DAY SEVENTEEN
Reading: JOHN CHAPTER 17

NOTES:

DAY EIGHTEEN
Reading: JOHN CHAPTER 18

NOTES:

DAY NINETEEN
Reading: JOHN CHAPTER 19

NOTES:

DAY TWENTY
Reading: JOHN CHAPTER 20

NOTES:

DAY TWENTY-ONE
Reading: JOHN CHAPTER 21

NOTES:

58615668R00064

Made in the USA
Columbia, SC
25 May 2019